Sleep Between
The Lost Dreams

Ignatius Maximus John

ISBN 978-93-5667-030-3
© Ignatius Maximus John 2022
Published in India 2022 by Pencil

Contributors:
Editor: Mon Maya Mongar

A brand of
One Point Six Technologies Pvt. Ltd.
123, Building J2, Shram Seva Premises,
Wadala Truck Terminal, Wadala (E)
Mumbai 400037, Maharashtra, INDIA
E connect@thepencilapp.com
W www.thepencilapp.com

DISCLAIMER: *The opinions expressed in this book are those of the authors and do not purport to reflect the views of the Publisher.*

Author biography

Ignatius Maximus John is a poet who has been writing for decades. His poems are filled with deep emotion and personal experiences that make his work relatable to many people. He writes about love, heartbreak, and the everyday struggles of life. He often writes about his love for the beauty in nature, which makes his work a beautiful read. He has been published in many magazines and journals, and has won many awards for his work.

CONTENTS

Dedication 10

The Poem 11

Death OF The Calendar 12

Broken Strings 13

Speedster 14

Bullet 15

Bite Me... 16

In Time 17

Frozen 18

Square.. 19

Colours... 20

Empty Spaces 21

Divine Masterpiece 22

Fate.. 23

The Play 24

Dilation 25

Trapped in Time... 26

Singularity 27

Happy Birthday 28

Pretty Blackhole 29

Death of Despair.. 30

Mach 20 31

St.Cloud 32

Back Again 34

Backyard 35

Broken Wings 36

For Woody St.Cloud 37

One 38

Plastic 39

Scream 40

The Best Comes Bad 41

Underoath 42

Young Blossom 43

Broken Heart 44

Drop and Hold 45

False Arts 47

Glorious Domicile 48

Limn 49

Questions 50

Reverse Acrostic 52

Shit 53

Wine 55

Die Alone 56

Now 57

Not For Each Other 58

Corridors of Fate...59

Demolished 61

Lost..62

Shadow..63

Show Her...64

Wonder of the Night..67

Stage 69

Lines From a Bard 72

You..74

Losing Winner 75

To the Stars 76

I Will...77

Honeybunch 78

Spell..79

Wastrel Songbird But Not a Bard 80

Forebode of Lines From Imbecile 81

Should Never..82

From the Horizon to the Stars 83

Tail..84

Coding...85

Epigraph

I swear, you could create galaxies with the stars in your heart...

Preface

"Fate is Strange " Sometimes it offers all aspects of what you expect, but it also denies you one when you need it most. Life is what our Creator gave us, but survival is something we must do ourselves. When it comes to tackling falling rocks and clearing trails, life can't be worth living if it doesn't contain the one thing you need.Emotionally tearing, tumbling, and crawling, we constantly worry I hold onto things. Heartache and despair always choose to stay indoors. Listening to the chirping of birds, watching the river flow, feeling the nature, and seeing the blue sky, my heart does not want to run away, I want what I want, so I want to relax. You can not. The book, Sleep Between The Lost Dreams, is about what it means to say "Fate fell short".

Ignatius Maximus John
IM Ville, 2022

Dedication

To my favourite person, I miss you everyday…

The Poem

An imperfection in the perfect plan

Trouble, woes and hardship are there

Mirth nay, sweet heaven, they

Forever lost in the desert we are

A paradise lost in their hands

The grand discrimination in the Master's plan

Or is this just a touch to the never ending story?

A static in the balance, seems perfect, eh?

The flow with flaws still flows

The great partition runs with the clock

The plan that has been already, but designed to blame

And the fillers, everything's there

An end before the beginning

Well done!!

Death OF The Calendar

We're never meant to be-
We could never be
There's never us only I
The wall's too high to climb
There's never a path to walk
Dead end cliffs on both ends
And now, I'll just watch her bloom

Broken Strings

Claims it to be her's

Drifting he far away

Wandering here she

Flying away there he

May be rapscallion he's

But white chocolate he hated

And pink butterflies may be

He loves cookies but only a cookie

Life that fade away in a grave

Broken strings never played that tune again

Minstrels once played that song

Never heard from the far land

Black rainbows loomed over him

The strings, it was broken long ago

But the tune still lingers in him

Speedster

Not a jump or a run, flying it is

Salyut and even ISS are lame

Absolutely defying gravity

Killing timeline in a blink

Rampaging The Flash

Even Reverse Flash's late

Bullet

Bollywood the shit outta me
And for the first time
I won't care what goes through me
Visions after visions
And don't you miss me twice
Or suspend my motion, if you will
Time after time
The big picture will hang

Bite Me

Closer than the brain

Traveling faster than blood

Oxygen and you are life

Tear out the skies

Drink from the clouds

Eat the sun alive

Bite the stars

And paint the town beige

In Time

I ricochet between the hands
Endless loop rotationg
The void that is full of nothing
Gravity, wrap the empty spaces
Set ablaze the water again

Frozen

Ever revolving through
Frame adds up
Wave in my sense
Frequency in my hand
To thaw the fire

Square

Frozen in time,

You're there

Atoms, 14 billions through

Space and time,

Now and forever

Sacred biochemical reaction

Days and years, lemniscate

Constant factor with perpetuity

Colours

Beautiful day for the beautiful faery

Sun and moon perfectly aligned

Let the mountains echo my thoughts

And winds whisper my name

Stealthy into your heart

As I filled the skies with the thoughts of you

Empty Spaces

That nothing

Without vibrating particle

Binary frequency void

Null particle and wave

Dark side for the world

Incremental nought

This nothing animates

Soul, life and this emptiness

Another dimension, heart

And my happiness

Divine Masterpiece

Mathematical plane,

White dragon

The jewels clutch and a jewel

Flying high,

Soft soul in the hardcase

Fibonacci sequence,

Golden ratio

Signature of God,

1.618 if you will

Perfectly perfect mistakes

Static fluctuations,

Structure of everything

Two tenses,

The noun and verb

Time and beyond infinity it will

Fate

Colliding worlds,

Orbital entry

Heaven's fated,

Beyond supereon

Unified diversely,

Silent hearts

Never will wither sacred essence

Kindled the eternal flames

Unfazed by the space and time

The Play

Nothing matters,
It's like an atom
Now and will be,
Vaccum and blackhole
Gravity and nuclear force won't alter
Void of senses and waves won't
Souls that transcend earth
Void cannot defy

Dilation

Beyond grasp,

Lock in time

Enzymes and reactions,

Loop eon

Precious atoms,

Perfect acid

Silent silence behind perfect silence

Already begins without the beginning

Trapped in Time

Speak of the sacred word, Faery

Tell me and end all this silence

Clear the doubts in my mind

Help me get over the past

And make me soar again high in the sky

I need that word, the word that would

Set me free from this chain

Speak now and whisper the sacred word

Singularity

Rainbow signals,

Deafening whispers

Dust of lights flashing through

Can't seem to pierce the singularity

But shines darkly in the pitch black

Glimmer of wave behind the particles

Keeping the hope alive for

One single unifying equation

In space where the void is full of nothing

That precious and eternal nothing

Escalating the reaction in all the time frame

Happy Birthday

Enchanting, serene and holy this day is
Sparkling and shining more than all other 364 days
Twilight, super moon even yuletide looks lame
King and queen of the calendar this day is
A perfect day for the perfect Faery
Days and nights you shine in everlasting light
Universe you light up, my Alpha Canis Majoris
Heaven's always be where you are
Colorful and loud words at the sky for you
Happy Birthday,
Faery, kwopkalawo'li…

Pretty Blackhole

Devouring waves, particles

Everything and even nothing

Can't escape the gravity

Electrochemical reactions

Getting reconstituted and

Reemerges in variation

Orbital entry not possible now

All the data got lost in oblivion

Death of Despair

Got the well full of coins

Plucked all the petals

Blown out all the candles

Never a day that I didn't

Spoke to the wall

And shot the stars

Not a thing that I didn't

Still waiting for the waves

Mach 20

Standing on the crossroad

I gotta choose forever or never

This gravity is too strong

Saw a light passing through

A comet in the solar system

I'm a comet chasing a comet

Frozen in time, chasing the clock

I gotta fly back in time

But I'll be burning too fast

I might turn into ashes

St.Cloud

The wind blows again and
I'm blown away again
But I'll sail in the sky again
The sun will shine and
I'll glitter high up again
Nothing can make me fade away
Wind, rain or whatever may

I was dancing in the sky
Laughing my heads off up high
Bestowing showers on her
Watching every move, every hour
Plighting our troth every second
Sending heart shape rains to her
As I sank deeper into the Love's pond

Lo! Now she's glowing in the sun
Relishing every beam from him
Driven away by the glowing rays

But still she not run

She dance in the rain in my rim

That made me locked in a maze

But St.Cloud I am and I'll be forever

Back Again

A forgotten desire back to the mind

The fade away dream back to the dreams

A past revisited in the present moment

The old smile back to the face again

Backyard

Back to the old school backyard

Where all the forgotten past dwells

The big eucalyptus trees no more

No kids jumping around and wick anymore

Lost footprints imprinted in the sand

Many come, many go not leaving a trail

Marbles, balls, big and small found no more

Sounds of joy and laughter vanished in the air

Silence echoes throughout the corridors

Dust in the air, spider webs on the walls

Broken bench, messy classrooms and broken chalks

Names carved on the window panes

Tables lying on the floor, broken chairs

Painting and pictures upside down

Empty atmosphere on all the rooms

Our lives got set here many years ago

But now no lives, but living memories

Broken Wings

You're hurt down there,

Just as I want it to be

I'm a psycho, I'm a freak

I don't care about her or others

I just want it bad

Like you could never think of

The fire will burn you

And set your heart ablaze

Like you're never before

You claim not to feel anything

But the truth is hiding in your eyes

And your lips taste horrid

Every failure tastes sweet now

You thought you'll fly, but you won't

Fuck your broken wings

For Woody St.Cloud

The worst cocktail of all

Happiness and sadness

It was fun then, almost death

Dad went away without going

Again we hit the block

Roses, cakes and whiskey

Pop went away this time

Started scraping the bottom

Welcome two this time

Walking backwards and been stripped

Themes of sadness and whiskey, songs

A little star appears on the horizon

Happiness amidst sadness

Worst cocktail of all

But St.Cloud I am and I'll be forever…

One

One from two and many from that
Life and life withal to lives
One road, the other road and many roads
Here, there, somewhere and where
Small, big, short, tall and every kind
Black, white, yellow, red and color
All from one and all to one
All under one, all under one

Plastic

Dying voices, undying voices
Heard and ignored together
'twixt their life and death
In this big Plastic world
There's no lives in the
Life of Plastic men
Doing so well badly
In this square circle
Lifeless life of the Plastic

Their terrible lullaby
Soothes their manufactured
Recycled plastic lifeless living
Babies to sleep
While their streets are filled
With their terrible cracking of the plastic
They smashed and broke themselves
But they recycled from that broken plastic

Scream

Fading melodies, dying lines
Silent cries, departed lovers
Silence screams, love tortured

Flying away from the heart
Leaving a trace of sadness
Thoughts bottled up inside
Pain in the heart, agony for the soul
Every bit of heart carved with memories
It was short but long
Sadness and happiness, vows and betrayal
Death of the undying love
Where vows vanished
And betrayal blossoms
The spirit it fades away, but it not
Love's locked up in the dungeon of the heart
Though it's eternal it dies
Or it's the fade away of eternal love

The Best Comes Bad

The foolish, but fullest

Had he gone with no gold!!

How sad the best is bad!!

Fiery elements but fine

Drowsy firmaments, but cool

The deepest measured by none

The worthiest comes worthless

The Prince with the rusting crown!

The blundest sword he wore

Filthy, but the seal of Prince

Swinged but veiled and hid

Beneath the dirty cloth

Adios if you had to...

Alas if you wish to...

The golden poet

The shineless diamond

Lost lost lost lost

The messiah by Jews

Underoath

He saw her. She saw him.

Different tongue but same heart

They sowed what they got and it nurtured

A traveler and a traveler, home they went

Through the invisible lines with words and voices

Traveled again they and happened again

Walked their home

He stepped out from under oath

She died from today, crying

Then, one from two but he denied

She's forsaken with the bud in her hand

He again under oath but other

She - lonely still waiting for him…

Young Blossom

Young blossom set to bloom
But plucked by death's cold hands
Why when there's many dying flowers
Did God's Angel pluck you?
To let you bloom, lovely in heaven

Your days of blossom were counted
But now you'll bloom for eternity
In my heart, our heart, their heart
Forever and for eternity
You'll bloom, my lovely blossom

Broken Heart

Tonight I groan and wail

From deep inside my heart

Sorrows and sadness surround me

Will I ever sleep again?

How could I walk through this?

No hope for happiness and love

No one's on my side

Everyone betrays me

I'm sick of the lies

But how can I make her believe me

Silver tongue, my enemy has

But me, I've got no words to say

This tension is killing me

Everyone shoves the lies to my face

How could I get rid of this burden?

Hate burns inside me

But I can't do anything

And I won't do anything

As I know the truth stands still

Drop and Hold

The scars won't vanish

The wounds won't heal

I just need a break

I won't get rid of it

All's after me now

I just need a way

But I can't choose

I need a drop and hold

The first can be the last

But the second can't be the last

I want the second

While I need the first and

I can't drop one

Nothing can fix, but

Ruin and break will

Can't let that happen

I'm in a dilemma

May be more than

A dilemma it seems

I won't drop, won't break

And I'll wait for anything..

False Arts

I glanced at the stygian sky and me sigh for lay knoll like
arose

Then I read poesy from so called wean bards

'twas a relished may be grieved loss

But if the while I think in those false arts

It annotate to me that every mortal fought for so called
fame

And exhibit they spurious abhorrent creation

Which made them only humiliate and shame

Entwine with fret and cease of determination

From then, only The Grand prosper and partiality begans

Masters are exalt while imbecile are disdained

The worthy of extol fords to the world where glorify
happens

And strived to protect the site they obtained

The great men forsaken with leaving a great piece behind

Which shines continually from yore in mind

Glorious Domicile

Erected with contrive of them and August's power of up
yonder

Stands on the dell where commence of credence from yore
still bloomed

Prosper 'twill for eternity I wonder

Desirous as they wait for the glorious domicile to unveil
afore doom

Surmise it to a boon for thee and I

Apace they toiled like the cloud which stealthy vanished so
fast

So as to cease the lack of the thing they sigh

And to apprise we of the requisite and to congregate for
mass

So be delight and rejoice with all this and be

Devote to thy preceptor and forget thy naive

And hark to the discourse of thy master and see

The momentus of their words so to rave

Let thou waited the unveil of the splendid abode with exult

With a soul filled with great assault

Limn

Little well-nigh of Albion I know
Accursed lineaments, wastrel it whisper
Wayfarer infront of thee I bow
Globe, isle thee drift like a mariner

Apprise we of thy lucre and thy ire
Erected thy domicile of marmoreal
Glorious preceptor feed me thy fierce fire
Black flag and lachrymal is all we yield

Descry thee despoil that nature bestows
Like cadaver we hark to thy discourse
That hath entwine me soul to lachrymose
Me devote not to thy words and thy force

Delight with forebode of limn from grand naive
Grieves hath I o'er me virtue as thee waste
Devote and hark to my limn so to rave
Beauty within and not beauty in face

Questions

Am I unworthy to be loved?
Is my heart unable to break?
Am I unable to feel pain?
Is my life a playground?
Am I born numb?
Am I born without a heart?

Why am I forsaken, while he's being loved?
Why is he worthy to be loved while I am not?
What was my mistake?

I was just loving and caring while he deflowers you
I was your friend and your lover
While he's just a friend.

Did you lie to me?
Did you lie?
I can accept and forgive all the wrongs you did
But why did you leave?

I can forget That night
But why did you go back?

Reverse Acrostic

Read these lines, it's reverse acrostic
Don't care what I write or do
May be I'm heading towards doom
Can't make it right what I'd done

Humans ain't like a Taxi cab
No matter if it's London or LA
Whether they're beggars or academic
Everyone has something that we lack

I wished there's some hope left
Now everybody got something to do

Don't say the work's assigned to them
Let's unite and act as one

Shit

Words I scribble, pictures I paint

Birds I like, nature I love

Cigarettes I smoke, whiskey I drink

Girls I like, women I love

Kiss I like, sex I love

Love I cry, hate I fall

Pictures hurt, memories torture

Mind damage, heart kills

Fire of memories burnt me alive

My heart is a monster

My mind is a devil

My body is just a worthless shit

My name's just a trash

I'm a slave of my own

Nothing's good, everything's bad

I'm not me anymore

I bleed every second

The game's played me

Tattoos digging my flesh

Everything's upside down
In this worthless life of shit

Wine

I drank wine from another man's bottle

Though sweet it tastes on the tongue

My heart felt it hard to taste as it was before

I'm lost somewhere I didn't really relish

I drink it only to quench my thirst not like before

When I drank to the fullest of my heart and all..

Would I ever drink again from another man's bottle?

I wonder and wander through every hour

Hard to stop drinking

As wine had entwined my heart forever

Am I worthy to drink only the left over?

Should I blind my heart and get a new bottle on my own?

Die Alone

She won't come back

Like no rivers flow back

He's left alone to die

She won't come back

To put the pieces back again

And nothing will heal his broken heart

Now

Will you just let me go?

Will you just set me free?

I'm tired of being sad

We're in the present

Not that gone hard past

I'm sick of you

I'm totally sick of you

I'm living a new life

Can you just leave me alone?

I've got nothing for you now

Not For Each Other

We hook up real late

Now I wanna change my fate

Don't wanna be burn by the hands of time

My life's locked and ended in my prime

I'll never kiss the butterflies again

Now I watch the stars and moon in pain

Will I ever kiss the sky again?

I'm blown away by the winds and falling rain

Corridors of Fate

Everything was perfectly planned
I just stuck to the plan and her
You're just the part time for me
We all knew we could never be
But think back when we get started
There was nothing wrong with me
But you're a floozy who pretends like an angel

Never thought I'd be shit to them
Pretty fake smiles and pop up face
Devil's book and swindled cash
Morbid thoughts and castle in the air
Was all that you got

I never thought you'd fallen in love
When you're just fucking around
I never wanna hurt you
Fucking sorry, I had to;
Never wanna put you this way

But you're always pulling and

Pushing me through

The corridors of fate

Demolished

Your past is killing me inside
You should have stayed away from me
Your kisses are hurting me now
You should have told me the truth
Now my heart is fucking me insane
You should have told me that you're floozy
You're torturing my soul
You're ruining my tomorrow

Lost

We stand in between now and then

We're close to the right time and place

Just a little something pushed us apart

Stupid words and fruitless fruit were holding me back

A little mistake was pulling me away

I never drift, it pulls me away from you

Bad luck enough to prove a disaster

You always grabbed my hand

Everytime I'm drowning in the water

Sorry, the last time I couldn't grab your hand

Shadow

I asked the wind where clouds have gone
Left the sky all are blue tone
"Why you asked, is there something wrong?"
No, just need some grey for my song

To ease the pain out of my soul
And may be the haunting memories
That hath made me become
A shadow of someone else

Someone strange, someone beloved?
Or someone who left me hurt?
But, that shadow embraced my crush
Graceful touch dropped on my painful heart.

Show Her

Forget the poise

Make some noise

Tell her how you feel

Peel away the layers

Of "Just good friends"

This isn't the message

You want to send

Get under her skin

For fuck's sake let her in

And tell her how you feel

You can't expect her to guess

This game of chess

Is anything more than real

Hold her hand

Make her understand

Where it is you want to be

What it is you want her to see

In you

That you are the person who

Sleep Between The Lost Dreams

Wants to be with her
Wants to share with her
The sunshine and the flowers
The laughter and the showers
Stormy weather
Together
Good times, bad times
Sometimes sad times
Wipe away her tears
Until the sunshine reappears
Accompanied by joy
Show her you are the boy
She's been missing
While softly kissing her cheek
Stroke her hair
Whisper
The future is there
Waiting
Anticipating
A joining of hearts
This could be the start
Of a lifetime as one
Hold her
Let your arms gently enfold her
Drawing her to you

Allow her to see through

Your cover

Open up

Become her friend and

Her lover

Be honest

Respect her

And never expect her

To be on time

Don't worry

Don't try to hurry love

After all it isn't a crime

If you have to wait

Does it really matter if you're late?

As long as you get there

Together.

Wonder of the Night

The beauty of the night is enhanced by the great lucent
silver moon.

Adorned by the myriad of stars across the sky,

Delighted by the soft blowing breeze with a pleasant tune,

Glorified by the wondrous nature that cannot die.

Descry I, think of a distant valley with gleaming light,

I entwine with maudlin, my soul, then forsake my body
thrice.

I drift and fly with slow grace, looking for a wellspring.

I gaze upon flowers and trees blossoming with a runnel on
their side.

But my soul forbids me to enjoy the beautiful woods and
the stream.

Then, I soar again, high up in the sky, searching for my
heyday.

But it made me sad when I realised that only a dream
could enable

I stared again I'm at Aether, looking for a way out.

But nature hinders my desire with her glorious state.

I ponder the things of the past.

My mind pursues and opens the gate.

of things that vanished as quickly as the spume.

which has caused me to wail with grief and laugh with
mirth.

And it elucidates how short we bloom.

It occurs to me that striving for a life is tough.

But all we have to face is our day of doom.

Now the moon is hiding behind a dark cloud.

Hide its ray of light in the hills and woods.

which made the melancholy crowd, waiting for the light,
shout.

made them exhume all their feelings from the roots.

I fly away from the moon and the cloud of serenity.

Then I swirl round and round with slow celerity.

Drifting deep into the pulsating dell

Passing through the woods and flowers

Unravelling the mysteries of the vale

As they waited for the blessing of showers

Stage

Are you

still

faithful

or

am I

still

faithful?

I

don't

know

why but

I can't

trust

you

And

I can't

trust

myself

May be

you

hate

me

or

you love

me

I don't care

much

but

I

really

love

and

hate you

May be

reality

is just

a stage

for

you

but

for me

reality

will never

be a

stage

and stage

will never

be reality

Lines From a Bard

How would mortals ever cease staring at thy beauteous
face?

How would nature ever cease sloughing its exult to thee?

Without thee, life is worthless and akin to living in a maze

So, every mortals would flail across any barrier for thy
delight and see,

They'd traverse thro' myriad of denes and mere for
winning thy hand

But all hope of courtship declined when young lad from
north vanquished thy heart

And let them to pool of ire with their hope vanished in
sand

But when sight thee revel the sweet spirit of love, rejoice I,
a bard

Let thee make thy love blossom for eternity

And offer orison to August of up yonder for blessings of
myriad

Mar the rites which turmoil the minds and let only love
prosper for marrowy

Forbid other wench to ravage the love 'twixt sans tirade

Thee hath left me vagrant and despoil my virtue nimbly

But shalt relish the longing and sadness of thee by
vainglory

You

And I had been patching the universe

Devouring worlds that rebels

Sending dark matters into blackhole

Collecting waves and rays

Keeping everything from colliding

Letting the flow flows without flaws

Losing Winner

If you ever feel hatred for me, you'll realise it's pointless.

I'll never hate you.

If you ever consider competing against me, you will realise
it is pointless.

I will never compete against you.

But when you realise you've lost a friend who truly cares, it
hits you in the gut.

When you realise you are exploiting others

because of selfishness and the desire for glory

It is never successful.

Peace begins with a single step.

Life is too short to be conceited.

If you ever need me, please let me know.

The worth of humane humanity, even if you're tired of it

If I could, I'd welcome you with open arms.

I wish you the best of luck in your future endeavours.

And my God will continue to direct my steps.

But, if you will, think twice.

What kind of joy and happiness does it bring you?

When you injure your friend in order to win the race?

To the Stars

Grateful to God in your darkest moments!

Because I was able to console you

Now, smile and let me wipe away your tears.

Whatever you do, wherever you are!

My feelings will always be with you.

I wish I could stay by your side on these cold, silent nights!

Unwanted reminiscences of the past

Something that was not supposed to happen...

Don't worry! Everything is going to be fine.

Obstacles are meant to be overcome in one's lifetime.

Never surrender to the darkness.

Try to forgive...

Come, let me hold you...

I'm extending my hands only to you.

We'll get through it together...

I Will

I will wait indefinitely...

I am certain.

I wish to remain with you!

All of us...

The breeze changed like nothing I'd ever experienced before.

This sensation is exclusive to you.

This is something I will never let go of.

Honeybunch

Little one, young and lovely...

Don't give up.

This is not the end!

Fight back...

We wanted to see your lovely smile.

We are happy if you are happy.

When you are hurt, we are hurt.

Get well soon, little one.

Spell

You've added meaning to the pages of my life...

My heart speaks your name with every beat. Words alone cannot express how I feel about you.

They are etched deep within my soul.

Wastrel Songbird But Not a Bard

Sung me not with contentment

Jest of the wastrels from yore

They so called exultation;

Grand Poser's disenchantment

So it with my heart they tear

Made I blithe with discretion.

So called award from cravens

'Poet of the Century'

Bestow they to the songbird!!

Blessings may be from Heavens

But all that makes me stormy

For to bestow to a bard.

Me mourn with lachrymose

For they waste mundane Bard's isle

And exalt fibber songbird.

All that they yield is black rose,

Me will never reconcile

Who writ no poesy like bard

Forebode of Lines From Imbecile

Me reckon that ludicrous lines from that fell, fibber,
wastrel imbecile

Whenst descry me, this hostelry jest from the sire of deride
isle

At once, repine I and mourn the woe with lachrymose, the
sin of idiocy.

Scoff I at this base bairn who akin to a barque sans
mariner in a mere,

For, this feeble minded gallant bruit this ludicrous jest.

Me disdain thee, for to read my poesy with peer

So, to be exalt, be my scholar 'til thee let thy soul to rest

Thro' this, thee could forsake thy hag-ridden of dread of
my poesy

Give heed to my words for thee could be accursed for life
and beg for my mercy

Should Never

The silence held us together.

We talked, but not about what was important.

We knew we weren't meant to be, but...

We are not allowed to. We could never do it together.

Life can be perplexing, but we are not.

The wings were too small and frail to carry us both.

We couldn't and won't be able to break the chains.

We always walk behind each other, but always together.

The walls were too thick and sacred to be breached.

The road is too long to walk down.

Miles were too far apart, but we're almost there.

The leaves and flowers cannot coexist for long.

We knew we couldn't and shouldn't, but we were certain of
the unspoken love.

From the Horizon to the Stars

We fall to the fall and it fall

The blue sky and the scattered clouds

Chill in the air and cold winds

Getting on a track like never before

Sidelines the heart and likes

But all the authority is there

This zone is strange

Everything and nothing is possible

No fate and fate walked together

I can be but i cannot be

I can wait but cannot wait

From the horizon to the stars

Always together in our own rockets

Tail

I'm a comet chasing for a comet

All around the solar system

I can't let you fly away

I'm lost in this Milky Way

I'm heading towards Andromeda

I'll search all through the universe

Just to fly with you everywhere

Coding

I'm caught in the shadow of romance

There's a glitch in the matrix

A typo in the coding it seems

A bug in the system if you will

Wearing my heart out on my ankles

Dirt, everything got in the way

This is not what i signed up for

Let me turn back time

And reverse the process